BIRDS OF A FEATHER
AND OTHER AESOP'S FABLES

RETOLD IN VERSE BY

TOM PAXTON

ILLUSTRATED BY

ROBERT RAYEVSKY

MORROW JUNIOR BOOKS

NEW YORK

Ink, watercolors, and acrylics
were used for the full-color art. The text type is
12-point ITC Garamond Book.

Printed in Singapore at Tien Wah Press.

1 2 3 4 5 6 7 8 9 10

Library of Congress
Cataloging-in-Publication Data
Paxton, Tom.
   Birds of a feather and other Aesop's fables /
retold in verse by Tom Paxton; illustrated by
Robert Rayevsky.   p.   cm.
   Summary: An illustrated retelling in verse of
ten fables by Aesop, including "The Laborer and
the Nightingale," "The Frogs Choose a King," and
"The Horse and the Donkey."
ISBN 0-688-10400-2 (trade). —
ISBN 0-688-10401-0 (library)
1. Aesop's fables—Adaptations.   [1. Fables.
2. Stories in rhyme.]   I. Rayevsky, Robert, ill.
II. Title.   PZ8.2.P39Bi   1993   398.24'52—dc20
[E]   92-2909   CIP   AC

BIRDS OF A FEATHER

Once a man decided to buy
A donkey that had caught his eye.
A likely beast that seemed quite able,
The donkey joined the farmer's stable.
The resident donkeys all cried, "Hi!"
The newcomer snorted and passed them by.
He turned his back and chose a spot
With the laziest donkey of the lot.
The farmer took him back next day
And to his owner was heard to say,
"He will not do, it plainly shows;
I'm sure he's like the friend he chose."

Man or woman, cow or sheep—
We're known by the company we keep.

PEACE BREAKS OUT

One evening at four,
A lion and boar
Each came to the spring for a drink.
Each had a great thirst,
And who would drink first
Was something that caused a great stink.
They clashed with a shout—
Fierce fighting broke out—
It looked like a war to the death.
In battle they clashed,
As loudly they crashed;
It left them both gasping for breath.

While resting, the pair
Saw high in the air
Twelve vultures all circling in flight.
The fighters now knew
That one of the two
Was meant to be dinner that night.
"Come, friend," said the boar,
"Please *do* go before;
Drink deeply, and let me say why:
Far better that we
Should be friends, you'll agree,
Than feed those who merely stand by."

All vultures' hope of dinner ends
When enemies become good friends.

SEEING IS BELIEVING

An athlete there was who was not very good
And was frequently teased by his mates,
Till finally he traveled away for a while
To try life in friendlier states.
One day he returned from his journey abroad
Like a hero who leads a parade.
He gathered his rivals around and began
To boast of a jump he had made—
A wonderful jump, a spectacular jump,
A jump no Olympian could best,
As any eyewitness who might ever visit
This city could surely attest.

The preening young braggart fell silent at last,
Till somebody spoke up: "I vow
We don't need to wait for someone who was *there*.
Just jump. Do it *here*. Do it *now*."
The red-faced young chap couldn't do it, of course;
In shame he went slinking away.

Remember this lesson: When making great claims,
Be ready to *do* as you *say*.

THE LABORER AND THE NIGHTINGALE

A laborer lay one summer's night
And listened the whole night long
To a nightingale in a nearby tree
Filling the air with song.
The laborer was so entranced—
So pleased with what he heard—
That he rose and set a clever trap
And captured the singing bird.
"Your home shall be this cage," he cried,
"Instead of a chestnut tree.
Your beautiful song is mine alone;
You'll sing for none but me."

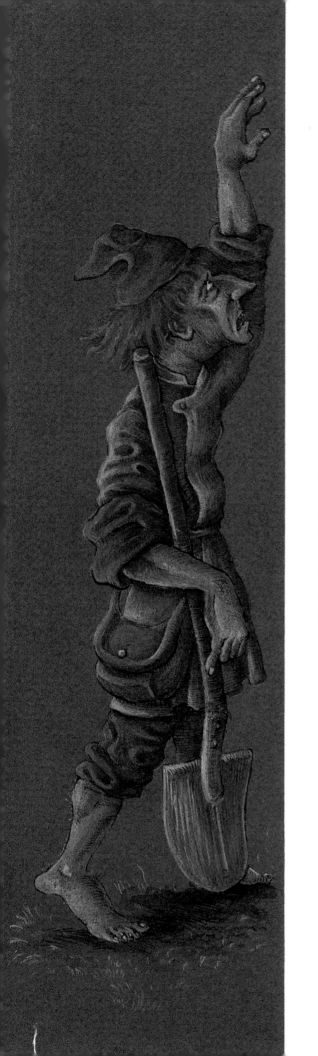

"You're wrong," the nightingale replied.
"You'd have no music then.
For a nightingale locked in a cage
Will never sing again."
"Is that a fact, my little friend?
Then here is how I feel:
I've heard it said a nightingale
Would make a pleasant meal."
"Don't eat me, sir, but free me now
And take some good advice.
Three pearls of wisdom I will share—
All precious beyond price."
The laborer let his captive go.
It flew to a nearby tree
And, settling its feathers neatly,
Said, "Now listen close to me:

Never believe a captive's oath;
It isn't worth a jot.
Second, you are always wise
To keep what you have got.
Third," he said as he flew away,
And the wide, wide river crossed,
"Never waste your sorrow, sir,
In weeping for what you've lost."

THE CAT AND THE FOX

The fox was boasting to the cat
How very clever he was.
"Just listen to me to learn," he sniffed,
"What a clever animal does.
I've hundreds of tricks to use," he bragged,
"When enemies cause me to run."
"That's so impressive," the little cat purred.
"My goodness! I only know one."

Just then the cries of the hounds were heard,
Ferocious and close as could be.
The cat didn't give it a moment of thought;
She turned and she ran up a tree.
"This is *my* trick," she called down to the fox.
"It's the only one that I've used.
Which one will *you* play, Mister Fox?" she inquired.
But the fox simply sat there, confused.
And while he was pondering—that trick or this?—
The fierce hounds came over the rocks.
He finally made up his mind, but too late!
And that was the end of the fox.

A hundred wild schemes might impress, but I say
One plan that *works* is what saves the day.

THE FROGS CHOOSE A KING

The frogs were happy in their pond.
They hopped, they swam with glee
Till one frog croaked, "We need a king
To give us dignity."
To mighty Jove they raised a prayer:
"Your praises, Jove, we sing.
Please hear us when we ask of you
To send us down a king."
So Jove threw down a mighty log.
It scared them half to death
Till one bold frog crawled up the log
As the others held their breath.
"It's not a king, O Jove," he croaked,
"Unless it's the king of logs."
So Jove sent down a stork instead,
And it started eating frogs.

Those foolish frogs ignored this rule:
Better no king than a king who's cruel.

THE POT CALLS THE KETTLE BLACK

A gray wolf was on his way homeward,
Dangling a sheep from his jaws,
When a lion leaped out of a thicket,
Snatching the sheep with his claws.
The angry wolf watched from a distance
As the lion went bounding away.
"You thief!" the wolf howled in his anger.
"That's my sheep!" was all he could say.
The lion just roared out his laughter
And up to the heavens it rose.
"I'm sure that *you* earned it," he snarled.
"It came as a *gift,* I suppose?"

One can't go wrong if one believes
There is no honor among thieves.

THE COCK AND THE PEARL

A rooster strutted round the coop,
Around the coop he'd go.
He proudly paced his bright domain
And, now and then, he'd crow.
His eye was drawn to something
Underneath a pile of hay.
"What's this?" he asked suspiciously.
"Is this my lucky day?"

But when he'd shifted all the hay
And cleared a space around
The object of his greedy eye—
A shiny pearl he found.
"Drat the luck!" the rooster squawked.
"It's very plain to see
You'd be a treat to someone else,
But you're no use to me.

You'd be a sight round someone's neck,
But, sure as I was born,
You'd find a greater welcome here
Were you a bit of corn!
You're not the object I would choose;
I value only what I can use!"

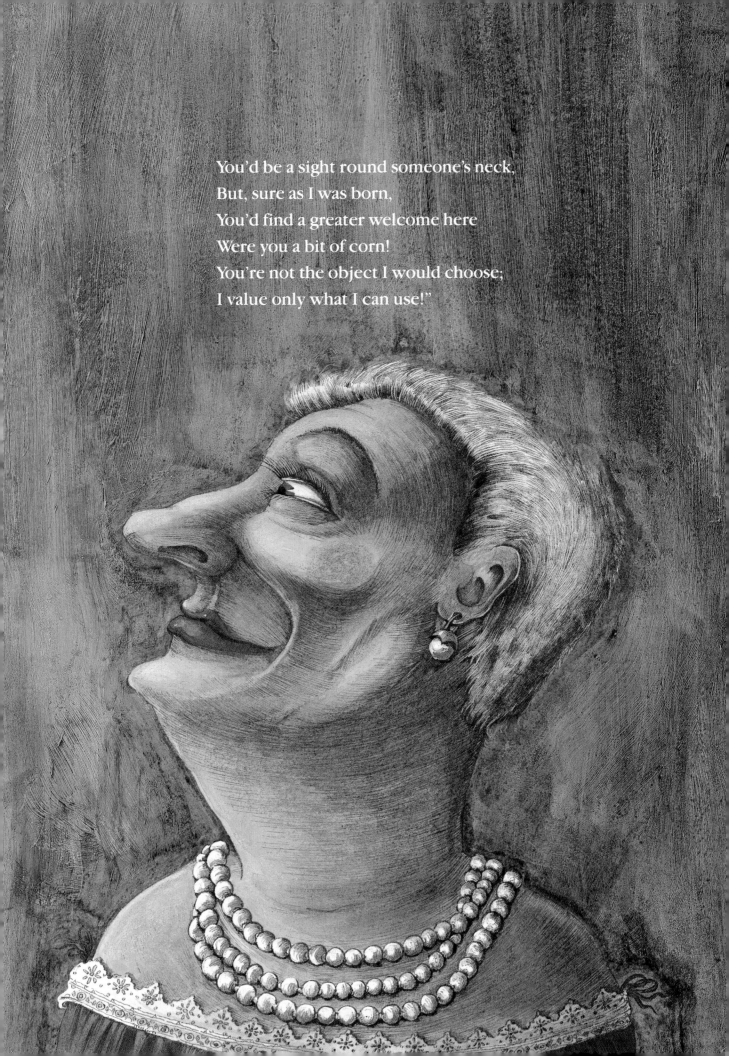

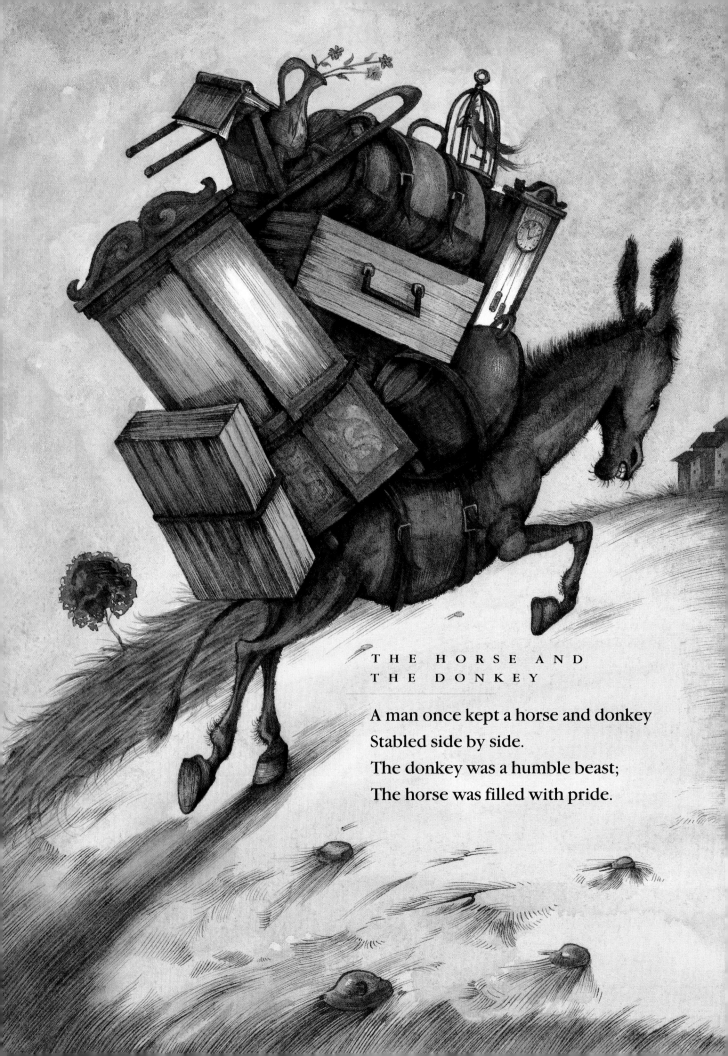

THE HORSE AND
THE DONKEY

A man once kept a horse and donkey
Stabled side by side.
The donkey was a humble beast;
The horse was filled with pride.

One day their owner went to town.
To market, to market went he.
He piled his goods on the donkey's back,
While the horse was allowed to run free.

The donkey groaned beneath the weight;
He staggered down the road.
"Kind friend," he whispered to the horse,
"Please help me carry this load.
If you will share this load today,
I'll soon be right, you'll see.
But if I get no help, this load
Will be the death of me."
The horse, however, tossed his head,
And whinnied in disdain.
The donkey sighed and suddenly died,
Finally free from pain.

Now, when the master saw this sight,
His anger I tremble to tell.
He piled the load on the horse's back,
And the poor dead donkey, as well.

The punishment was harsh but fair.
We must agree to do our share.

THE WIND AND THE SUN

The Wind and the Sun were both fussing one day;
It seemed that they couldn't agree
Which one was the stronger. They argued the point
Till at last the Sun said, "Let's see.
I have just spied a traveler down on the road;
The coat that he's wearing is gray.
Let's see who can make him remove it, my friend—
That will prove who is stronger today."

The wind began blowing; it bent all the trees.
It howled as it blew through the wood.
The traveler shivered and clung to his coat
And wrapped it as tight as he could.
The wind blew still stronger. It blew up a gale,
Determined to blow off the coat,
But the harder it blew, the more tightly he
Stayed muffled right up to his throat.

The sun began shining. The warmth of its rays
Beat down on the traveler's coat
Till he took the thing off and stood fanning himself—
Leaving the victor to gloat.

The lesson we learn is an old one, of course:
Persuasion will always do better than force.